Tomorrowland

Other works by Lisa Samuels include:

LETTERS (Meow Press 1996)
The Seven Voices (O Books 1998)
War Holdings (Pavement Saw Press 2003)
Paradise for Everyone (Shearsman Books 2005)
Increment (a family romance) (Bronze Skull Press 2006)
The Invention of Culture (Shearsman Books 2008)
Throe (Oystercatcher Press 2009)

LISA SAMUELS

Tomorrowland

Shearsman Books
Exeter

First published in in the United Kingdom in 2009 by
Shearsman Books Ltd
58 Velwell Road
Exeter EX4 4LD

www.shearsman.com

ISBN 978-1-84861-050-7

Acknowledgements
Thanks to the editors who published excerpts from *Tomorrowland* in
Damn the Caesars 4 (Richard Owens), *Hotel Amerika* 7.1 (David Lazar),
*Invisibly Tight Institutional Outer Flanks Dub [Verb] Glorious National Hi-Violence
Response Dream* (Ryan Dobran, Justin Katko, and Sara Wintz),
and *Landfall* 216 (Tim Corballis).

I am grateful to The University of Auckland
for a Strategic Investment in New Staff grant that helped foster my poetry
and to the Brown University Literary Arts Program for being my home
during the research semester when I wrote this book.

Cover image: 'Hieroglyphic Night', collage, by Camille Martin.
Copyright © Camille Martin, 2008.
Author photo by Tim Page.

Contents

The argument 11

It's all good 15

Treasure Island 22

Sirens 29

Neptune's open mouth 36

Bulwarks 44

Landed gently 57

A little history 64

All the buildings made of voices 72

The body's charge 84

Circumference 95

Further reading 99

for honest dealing, and for ship goers

You shall be my guide, she said, you'll be my argonaut, with you I'll go everywhere. I'll go into the cafés, I'll jump into the dives, I will enter into the *Passages*, I'll go through the oldest sections of the city. I will go into the slums, the two of us will march ahead through the night, forward, until no place remains that has not been trodden under our feet. I shall be your queen, you'll be my king, I will not be afraid, you will harbor no fear, I'll have no more nightmarish memories, you'll have memories no more, I shall be without a past, you'll be my future, you'll be without a future, I'll be your past

        Réda Bensmaïa, *The Year of Passages*

Thus in the beginning all the world was America

        John Locke, *Second Treatise of Civil Government*

The argument

The second difficulty is the sphere itself
As I plunk on an inclined plane
My cube pulls its little feet and heads for ground
For good measure under the skies in the bookcase
Next to the little bird whose banana choices
Are sublime in the extreme. Everyone has barometers
And I want to know quickly how contact terminates
A moral tone into two opinions of a brickbat
Whose charming lawns are multiply divided
Who have hanged peripheries so many years
We recognize sui generis the pattern of translated mourning
Skies, the introversion of outgauged handwriting
Preserving in its traces like the stylus generates
The outlines of our will transpired—the plane
Is leaving at this very moment by a little spiral
And a legendary decades task we talk about
Aggressive privacy and second-line defense lapels

The pretty men stroke so tenderly while their
Hard-working mothers also invent a wheeled
Circumference whose almost imperceptible sighs
Quite register when the four bumps hit the ground
The road assizes. You travel concordant lumps
Or bounds will little calm your tribute tree set down as
Mostly canopy for foliage founding, the mountains
Rising two by two within the ships whose every
Outlaid squad trips up a sweet cadenzian sorrow
We can plough.

We land to divination with our tongues in the water
Indeed the material world literally swims
With certain angles of (your face a range careers
they bear with them an ordinary day of handmade try
their lives appear and reappear in moments in a key
we were saving for the crux of our discussion
'life in public' work demands the ease inhabits not
only that such figures idle actively but you
among extremes will go with curtsies half-addressed)
The city's gazes looks and contact spills over the bodies
Talking shared unwritten sense
Wondering what the hurry was in a flower bed
Calling stalwart thirst intensified over glass
The vertical bell strikes six cessation think divide
Think ethos executes reformist zeal twinned
With a sail (for numerable countries) deeply of Arcadia
In half-gallon vigor to say to say that were as

(we were soft and pliable but still) monocultural suggests

The point a landscape rich for sociality (then hold my hand)

With Eula mobilizing narratives in a café

(where we sit with open arms) latent demand

To plug in essence grassroots spiralina

Semiotic (with a napkin) central sale did not exclude

New users like bi-folding hospitality toward the street

A wider public theatre employed (to bring us to repast)

This certainly is superior put to work (your tendrils

prominent display coordinates my eyelids you-ward)

While we parochial delicious turn the key the streetscape

Activists (and through all these encounters) the usual

Disclaimers well apply

It's all good

Well, initial profoundly
local to people a place where flesh engenders
remarkably pluralistic Eula gathering
bright currant cordials and itinerant pop
laid out in the capital working through
a metropolitan-inflected begin

So let us start the moral philosophy of focus
at home in the wider world of competence
and fit(ful munching fingers left
of travels in a state of readiness)
synonym for in situ seats
of such extremes as circle signs correct attire
quickly called a concentration and their struggle

(Thus both about the city we did stroll
themselves providing ethos sandwiches

inside our) social bonds
He is at pains to point, is actually generative
we need to think not local to it grid
the world a techno-scape in contrast to
your (own sweet) axis (given to applause)
This is an aspect barely touched upon

★

One day without horizon our green jackets might well chorus afternoon
A man a woman singing children in their milks arising
Out behind a crystal globe murked with colored water
That we lit at night when warmth degenerates the streets.
The full moon on his face he walks by beaches untranspired
Thin lips set against ideas of permission nor
More alley rushes disallowed here streaming.

The garden faces by a crack uneasily in its palm
We groove the red flowers rushing deep path flight
Our eyes most tender clip. The brown locks of the husbandry
Are puckish in their rust, we draw our index figure-eight
Nor touch it not a hot diurnal brand. Each day the furthest
Rustling of the ivory liked to call a dog a dog had brought
To soften all your green whips into ours. A cautious spider
Afternoon eventfully in clay molded a hand convulsed
Disturbed, he builds the little ship we fly up
Rose petals entrailing. One afternoon he cut the pages
Of his only book and found began to truly love.

This smacks of tom-tom mumbo jumbo permeable routine
So clean the flesh unrecognized, of pencil sheets more
Ravishments top down to down and follow.
Which are what interests us: asylum we have had
The meantime primal well remote and even physical objects
Interest us extreme. This city is of biscuit picture
Troped for brave response and dizzying beer is anamorphic
When it gets into his belly and unfurls. The initial
Hand-to-hand was well assaulted pictures of idea
Played out headlong in a dishy history—his metamorphing
Fauna could disturb us with their drawn incredula
Had we not firmly mastered middle distance.
Today the sidewalk spins with our remote
capacities and in the kitchen years are never
studied by Max Planck though we have written him
in firmly with a swaggard oath
technopolis gently follow.

What then of social being? Bodies gesture Western fleshy
Left-right orient, a transcendental island soft erasure
That is totally mental, dear, you see how filtered ambiance
Has left us here dynamic while we occupy and highlight
Each respondent: you have a form prognostically bereft
(before that is you even learn to take) of flesh and bone
To mortar acts and build. In a world you've left
Your feet behind you pretty agile drifted reverie
As though the maps were soft bread tread exploiting
The mundane. Look moss on slopes, look asphalt that

Suspiciously transfixes, the hall slapped out like wrappers
On the brevery domain. Your helmet is a kind of mushy
Pate with which you ruin the tranquility of texture:
Ohmygosh trees, flagrant birds in plangent urban oomph.
I mark you with my little x and you go all amen
Through new life durable as the salt whereby you heat
Your common use, a matter of space, a total fix
Inside the heretofore dubiously infiltrated corridors
Of water rather than toil or encounter with the
Widest sense—a caveat, a square, a built-up instability
We give each other several times a year exchanging
Physicality for idea every time.

The same different younger palimpsest's itself a reverie
Preoccupied with heavy trees the tresses of the customary route
In which your cities are so reverent smothered.
Formation builds a castle round your eyes and tells
Two devastating fires invested totally with limbs
And urban planning, I stroke you with the sand from sandy beaches
As if to forge forget the simple process abstract economics
In the field. The blitz has eyes reacts to this extremity
So follow, as your unraveled testament reminds me
With its too-short cavalcade and surgeon's wheel.
A curious act of total newness deified by its dissenting flower—
(you cannot smell the newsprint pressed up
to your face, pervading) every Eula's short-hand town
Best-selling semi-fictional and grey.

Archaeologists love rubbish, after all, and we can't tuck
enough of Scotland in our spoil haps, nor Yorkshire cattletrap
third-year Mexican rubbish art dance cart manual
transmission, Japanese embroidery, American solids
and all the island habitats so Wittgensteinian.
We need some digging surface to find lies below
we need some secret networks with which to build sincerity
pikes for all our aching heads. We need a bluet sphere
to calm our material surfeit of indemni-cards, Freud and void
having convinced us they are totally in love with everything we might
imagine self to be. You have to ask who owns what and why.
The view you can't have is like 'I understand.'
The residential barriers were all in place when Big Bird hatched
his egg colossal beam of sunlight on his starboard
acquiescent side not nullified fast enough
for everyone watching. I was personally inspired
by a topographic radio set breathlessly in the window
of a dying European architect—nobody wants to come here
for the self, I imagine, the sun surveys a wet fish shop,
a decent baker, and our hands glued continually faced out.

*

In the bluey sky a chorus of silent flitterings
Whose habits encourage us to look at our own
Nests and plans of worry—have we been here before?
Are we a nest of scarry flitterings? We can take over the whole page
And still the sky shapes pale so lovingly
As though we had a nurturing inclusion all along

In an oriental fold book whose cyclical motif

Suggests implied women throwing themselves

Over cliffs whose misty pictures cannot fully resolve

The concept of no beginning nor no end. This type of book

Cannot be arbitrarily selected in a line running mildly without panic

Through the failure of trains or welcome placement

In so time. Our Eula has a fairly lot of inner-city

Aliens to contend with, cordial beaches notwithstanding

The patter of lithe fleet upon their bones

Inspires a traveling philosophy whose major strengths

Are held in by the water at the shore:

Rock islands greenly cropped by swine we laid out

In the capital sublime as hungry conversation

Pushing for a crux of handmade try whose density

Might earn it the respect reformists long for—and

The white swells truly fathoming that clipped-off urge

To say to say the thread that's merely left us but

The end of which we dangle through our hair,

In front of our eyes, inside the pressing demographics

Of our new parochial counter, click click tell me mystic shipyard

How you otherwise match perfectly the ceremonial trees

Beside the bay?, would your fine planes make appetite

A total leaning toward stone fences whose every lifted muscle

Means the pretty men worked carefully then too?

A tribute fence invisible

surrounds the wild encampment

where defiant mourning gauges his barometers

so still, you might think young girls
bodies had been used to make the air
how gently it stirs trees toward a falling sky.
Everyone wants to know the channel moon
under the leaps without horizon definitely planned
—we lit at night a subterranean crack
whose promises unmeetable have us
silly with excited premonitions: we'll see
the other bridge they'll build some day,
container wharfs deep in the faith
they rustle for the silent dogs or looks—
encampment is another word
for broken circuit husbandry, not ivory but bone
you're holding there.

Treasure Island

All afternoon in cautious clay the island gurney ponders
Her existence, why she's diurnal singing from the wind
That interests us—though we can't see the morphic
Fauna driven through the keels, our ships are lavish
Gatherings whose every social being's made such plans.
You see we occupy the world you left with plaintive x's
Differential branches, the too-long soldered tilts toward
Those cities whose accumulations look at you
As though your generous glances stole this world.

Just as the messenger is part of the message I
obsessively check my maps, why doing this is not
an illogical supposition nor is the beach
holding either solely out nor in the tide
nor sand from each direction giving a priority to
another—how do you do?, or going I sometimes hear

and as if given persimmons I suck my answer
slowly in my mouth before considering—I think I'm going

Well, somewhere between the two. The color is always expected
to appear in some shade of itself, the sandy beaches furthering
the proposition laid inside my brain. Egg-like, I roll it over
cliffs that soft my fall with sand or gentle grasses
leading to another (that day we rolled inside the rushes
high on windy point, while everyone was lovely over there
we crept in nests and felt the green against
our face and hands eluting).

Artists have often felt involuntary fracture, like the hill
Garroted through with lusty planks, as if inviting the same
Entry to every fervent creature's dirt inside their mouths—
A curious newness in their eyes in love with acquiescent
Barriers mountains can put up (or so I hear
the dulcet visions of the southern ones and planning
with fidelity to the new, but I was saying tucked
here on the magnet side) with bone-revealing sunshine
Flooding out the place that people are so perfect ear-marked
Conduits the road between has forced them rather sexily
To make up and come over here, tide yourself a while
for evening's found a need for you, the street-side
wall against experience is electric.

★

The narrow runways
where the matted grasses
—the similar species grooved
economic—the platform home
range *faintly washed with brown—*
silvery to the slightly buffy
mammae branch appears in early
evening—*feeds on left hanging roost—*

and you, my grubs and tubers license
you are graceful furbearer shade
to gold, nomadic and monogamous
when you have the chance—field guide
our Manda sees inside the cells through
myriad cycles stored for later fragile
information eco-stuffed inside
your genesis, your writerly insertion
muted out from fostered form

Load home upon your tongue
and hold the warm composite
rolling out wide field inside
the clumped-up green that tickles
paths along the side where mud
translates some opposite non-unison
of which are wet and feet and pageant
moss contracts my walk

Writing imitates surfaces indigo basins feel
a present liquid social quality

on the retinue we make up gently
charm at a loss devising the same cups
those hills hide frondly steam and
mist the chilled air while we wait for breakfast

*

In keeping with the aims of generative contrast, the islands
Have regarded on and off for centuries
(although they couldn't know or cloud each other
with deliberation, even when feet *could* forfeit
rocky jazz exteriors wind extremes) and so we ask
Ourselves: What did we do and when?
Caustic stays set on the trees collapsed
But couldn't reach across the dire agency we pressed
Against their mouths (which having carved so woodily
were *in* a promised expanse for something like
each other's sake). Chromatic vigilance forestalling
All the bait we'd set in memory of St Martin's or of Rose
Street or the Transveldt Himalaya or 70% ocean
Waters you're welcome to employ
We'll wait for you our nets set wooden bait
While he takes his myth and puts it out there
In the literal sense, over again incorporating oysters
And their total inability to resist.

Decentralized agentive husks, the wooden ships
you're modeling for months on end like a pair of
words not wasting precious time, your false convictions
and my falsies gave the happiest news that each could

recommend. A third text weaving frames linguistic
troubadours who sing not to each other within hearing,
having landed their domesticated ships
with aches and prejudice intact.

I fell in love with time's indisputable eraser and used it to delete
my ears and toes. Thus paralyzed I fetched the resolution
given tongue's analectic fire (cool wet equation) given
platform's wedge between the aforementioned trees
(which having not managed island spaces still truncate
their doldrums past apology straight to rancor,
the tight quick press of work making that easy)
I was squeaking past of course imperial tires
but as long as I am good the sides will let me wait while
local prime scatologies pat each other down to see
who hangs the fastest mortal for his trouble

What happened was essential to my pried-out
Grateful to you nice about it lesson. After all,
Raleigh the alchemist told the whale to take his moral
To a neat knife numbed half-wickedly for Hume
The philosopher of relation. His medium had a blade
For maximal use, tradition joined argument so slowly and complete.
Thus coastal disproportionate form is hanging Jack
Poorly for his unplanned sup while we watch with our
Double tongues all doubly fetching out.

★

Insofar as two ways south are like this we are
Wet and clement and our science models can't help being as
Molecular discrete genetic viral microscopic
Plant-based, body-bound, playground, greensward
Beachy. Where am I from that arid permutations
deify my lists? Unsacrosanct one-ing what she said like
quanta mime. And I am there each chance I get
since (body heat's itself a form of argument or armor
dropped at slight provoking quests, such as I walk
and look and listen to the other talking with his gentle
mouth and I can only think. Darkness is another matter since
it is not here at all—it is never dark. The dark is always
cancelled by intenser dark at the hintermost belly at the
bottom of the island or the post-romantic sea whose
stark fidelities make all the people here shine out
like light sweet chancy evocations so they set each other
onward which I wander through though offering no unbid telepathy)
I see nothing that I see. Slenderizing baby talk progressions
Staking out some ways and oh coloniality thine art has made
Me brute with recollection.

*

If it weren't for Shakespeare we'd never have Jane Austen if not
For Milton no whales would ever rise up if it weren't for
Something tasting like belief we'd never hear the end of
Sad-sack loyalties like the proximate-to-fishes guys
I mentioned earlier, wanting us all to feel more
Comforted on the salty trail. The birds are still calling

With the attitudes that got them where they are today with
Freedoms we could take and take. The crackling
Of fires will announce you found arrival quite near to
Where the wet ground held its own proportionate
Aufhebung or common song its marvelous ontology
With recognizable feet stuck permanently in the sand.

(Way in)
The ants are subtle here, no larger than northern scallywags
whose every move shows forth their settled life amidst
large ants who eat them for a bridge—in both a matter
of fitting in to something, narrow paths of sugar that your tribe
lays out for you to suckle, little guy, and finding the right one
will get you everything you need so long's you stay with it.
The kind of advice any cultural information center gives
when you're not asking twisted in the entrails. But I was saying
the ants avoid attention here they place their little feet with
happiness. Although one time they swarmed like all
get out nor could I tell what they were baiting for—just more
invisible reward I guess that latched them to the hill
where chemical assembly was decided. A lovely self-
sufficient round and not so fraught as elsewhere I suppose.
Though maybe ants are trying to figure out amalgamations
of their substance where it leads—the shore,
the trees, buildings, life with other ants, or maybe
they could change the ruffles on their feet to ceiling stick survey
the full range of equipment this particular library wants
to have on offer. It isn't easy to decide.

Sirens

For I could be in love with you would let me to appellant
Forecaster, with crumbs along the trail around which
Animals are missing parti pris, a part from tangled webmasters
Provincial allocations hurt like salt (like blinded fathers
resting on their couches with their nightmare juices pickling—
a sea ensued from Eula's gallant unresolve), a whole set
life modeled after vacant ships whose keels lie
down in soft sand partly filtering, the diffident little armatures
of things relate to fishes for our furthermost protection
from the Jack. Her maw mowed moss malignant fallow
Frankly from the sea as though rised out from ornaments
That spilled over the side when yet another man was traveling
Hinterward—an incarnate and clapboard abecedarian foretold
That winches would hinge upward from the middle of the world
Whose belt was tightening by the day—we went to school
And learned that your predictions made no difference

After all the green May backward sacrilege, the shelf awaiting
All the bodies clamoring for the last long sip of tea
The last long armor fit the long last conversation
With the persons you would never last on attitudes
Whose culture came alongside so's you'd understand
A line when it was spoke—not that allegiance fell along
Your gallant rasp sauvage, your empty sofa gathering
Features that would background wane when absolutely
No one's looking for their eyes
are knotted cannon-like on featherdust
the boy promised the wall he'd be back
the girl promised her tree not to waste effort
the family carved its ink along its flesh to remember

Things rescened to pattern after all
these turns. There is no man named Jack here
though the parrots' gaunt survival might depend on it
befriended with a club held out
stalked with a lacy gauntlet we could call
our mate for life Expressions of Interest
ferried in from Nowheresville they noticed like
the banded curtains we observe along the equatorial
subsumed. (And tired the man held out for disposition's
parallel, you are not yet moved into that space wherein
your vertical obsessions make you live and breathe
and have your office all set up for optimal equations.
There are if anything too many ways to get the whole thing going
so it's better really when you think of culture as inherited and
good so less taxing so no Jack waiting in any fearful way

the great man parroting the revolution he can hold
now gently in the form of recent books.)

And yet we know that gentleness is potentially where it's at
that strong equation you can check each day inside
your edifice—or several serve to show you how
your buildings strung around you with indomitable ease

> *My documents are manumitted finally they talk to me in corners*
> *where I've patched the walls where little creatures have their way*
> *if I don't tend them manfully*

> *the highway signs are good for that I peel them off most carefully,*
> *hiding behind the green trees thicket and extravagant ragged*
> *glories.* This morning sliver moon left out on sky in sculpt

> last night old sun rolled backward down the water, my
> friends conjoined to parlay in the wonted house our
> voices tending wave-like toward the edges of the room

> where the aforementioned highway signs are shiny
> substitutions for the care I cannot lack, where little words
> encourage aforementioned friends to riff on substituted
> mileage posts consumer afternoon.

★

They came along this time the atolls
(Neptune's mouths) to tell the variations
Of the Sky Road story: a violent yoking of

Our pelagic syllables with

The porous baroque of sky

Resulting in a foot path that our children walk

> Around and around *and around and around and around without*
> *a sound they recognize as wellness operates to borrow from the*
> *sedimented caprice of what we're wont to call our own designs (too*
> *small they weigh in skeletal as moondust, collected pageantry of the*
> *driven missives of one era or another whose fine articles make powder*
> *sand a humming quantity when we hold it in our missal cups to*
> *brood) when rarely streets will curve toward the terminal escarpments*
> *of the sea*

whose able-bodied stipulates will gladly

well aware the servants come out here

your boys your love away an easy labor

stony bed provide eight hours of gainful need

enforced by round apartments.

The shock could stop his heart with new examples

The buffalo (e.g.) not here across the bookend seas

Which moved in harmony to wipe them out—we all put down

Our heads to knock polite distinction from this engine trace

Taking over in a penalized adjustment collage, consistent

Statements straitened out with sidewalks made of derivé

And sixpence shells stepped right inside a saturated non-set

Meaning context not this culture yet to take over the pulse

of water heat light particle clouds

steam black sand cream green trees

all image captured which the loose experience will arrange into

another stable run alongside so you hear that sound

Roll out, the click in space—

Fifty years ago I was in rural no profoundly

Disaffected without knowing about fear

An ur-insensitive license made the journey most extremely

Eula-speak, invisible to many the condition

For the surgical lurch dogmas and competing

Fragility whose drama would form the few percent

We could finally read at all.

The purity of your conviction

Solely of the broken tongues

For new minority follows.

(A hundred years ago) the nerves of Fasti's feet

Agree a doorlatch patiently apart

My patrimony truly far from home in a necessary

Curse protected from the distance of a fate

Whose perpetuity has heft and iterate objections

Hesitating on the conscience of a capture.

Our stakes are in ebullient humiliation all except

The skins we're filling out

The bands rewoven in some really

Voice-encapsulating trees

Engaged in both the offending child and its

Completely non-tragic

(because so answering back the birds and houses

conjugations of persons building each other so continuously

prisons nor their elite obscurity adventures taking risks

they can be socialized nay government and business somewhat species
in given-up heart histories whose clement cultural metaphors
will trespass a chain and rush the explanation
with their tongues transition secret
deciders giving each other the nation state
whose wrong recurrence writes the past
against available feathers stones leaves
bones words spiders
cut and paste more than anything we know
about someone else's) life because
If you're part of wholes then only fully destructed
Stuff be tragical exemplars
Never stripped of their belonging
Don't forget nothing is betrayed in an indicative mood

★

With image I am grave, with the body least
integrated in slopes to use again in the representative mention
of its times. I was waiting for Eula absorption to discover
the museum, despite the man reading in front of it with a cause
will have that same reaction in the imprints really about
ways to make your sign more like the one he carries
against the particular propositions of that house, its decisions
unaccepted as we no longer enter our new century.

Examples are not arguments: in an unbroken
series of declarations he convinced us that

responsibility was not our fault.
A mood swing was set up on the trans-
coded playground I notice, and the fire corn
seed laid out its fire corn seedlings while
the government administered the fields.
Don't think of alpha particles
don't suck old rocks in magnet snows
the warm and gentle schools will mostly
hold you, the backward wash of culture
unprepare your inborn stealth.
Pause here over the symmetry
and your little corn collapses while
the sea puts up its head wild flowers
in the forest carve you there inscripted history
an interrupted corkscrew opening the first
new bottle of wine not being yourself.

But take the lesson you were given and throw it over
your shoulder: it pays to be kind to ideas, for they
will never desert you never take your hand
and throw it over their shoulder because you have collapsed
never take your body and throw it over the hillside one fine day
when you become aware of objections to the turmoil where
your circumstances have desired you in accordance with
a new (obscure) modern mythology of a theory of needs
or romantic press of circumstance or the serial way in which
you dip your legs into your class just testing.

Neptune's open mouth

Under the tide my legs are musical
display on moonlit net
inside the recurrence of that water I
turn and turn my lavender
brought for company, a ritual
bonded to position symbolizing a brink
the river that defeats itself
so harmony so swallow
the salty body not able to be
contained in microscopic
sandy lacerations that I cover
with my sail skirt when I'm done

with those red frondy flowers gently
stickling the air saves up a sketch of flowers
ballasted with a pose
sudden as riff legs swallow

throats sing droplets from
the touching of the bird
to that frilled blossom entering the book.

My arms are numb and legs fixed
flutter sensitive to a light that turns
a temporary window well behind me
when I look a roofline into fronds
your go-go transit emigrated shades

★

Nothing is as it seems nor is it your scenario extruded
From your shirtfront onto paper trains
We set going down the country to attain the wherewithal
We kindly wrote to tell them—we are not designed to perceive
Majority rule but we must suck it up through straws
In our own reedy consequence, our bodies
Not designed to feel majority nor rule
An absent sway encouraged in fell trees

The very regularity in this saturated world ersatz strained imagination
Who's she talking to? A martianized origin media boom
In the same main stream narrow notions
Paradoxically fetishized in the inanimate reaches of
Creative mishearing. By now you're so expected in
Your movement charactered or are you one specific
Theory taken up to viewers text dynamics
With gestures of susceptible magnanimity: one

Coat hanger, two planks, and we'll be done with it.
We're trying to start tradition here
You see our love desire laughter whom
I recognize most thoroughly ensphered.

If a gradual hybridity brings us surfaces
will we actually just talk about ideas? My friend
centrally located in a print fracture—we tried to fit him
in a digital extent but the last few lines
conflate regretful pushing
—adjust yourself to lovely stones
that are totally settled insofar as
form permits a stop
both portraits are nicely anecdotal
fields that one supports by photo opportunities
like this intends as though a body
were included in the words by being next to them.

I walked and hence discovered I had feet
like yours I clubbed and saw the dancing was quite similar
I swayed and was the trees impending shapes
splashed into surf I felt the child's older water
straight impound my grip.

(Arrival's song)
The day you arrive you place hands

Light viscosity through a breach
From the boat your harbor sank
Into ideas of the first tall sense of totems
A form in the social realm whose habitus
You're made for as you spread out
All your papers and experience.

Impressionable space makes little clapboard
Arms crawling all over the new monuments
And giant steel promises hover there and there!
>   Most people in the world are dead, you know
>   *it intimate with your just-past huddle*
>   *in the difficult ship language scattering*
>   *dust over the edges into the glass jars*
>   *in which accumulate a little of*
>   *the death-sand from the sites*
>   *we fondled with our eyes*
Like stories we began to hear: a man calls his beloved
From the top of a hill and she being wind answers
Nothing but repetition through the years he keeps calling and
Becomes the tree that grows atop that kind of hill

A child drowns in the fresh water and we keep seven days
Without drinking for we know the child's fingers are beneath the surface
And wanting us for rescue on the eighth day we call out three times
The child's name the child's name the child's name
And we know the water has released its spirit through the sky
And we can drink again, our breath suffused with all
The little beacons of the child's spirit answering

We hear the story of the man who cannot stand
Himself arrayed inside his socius and he takes
The fine strong rope woven of the rushes
And he rushes himself away from himself
As fast as not raising his arms to help
Himself can do

They would not be able to realize it then
Fading on the aperture of the epics of this century
With particular flowers featuring as the last outpost
(like Roosevelt or the moon or ancient seabed
or the real arrival presence and the earthbridge overland
peoples starting in the forest where the tablets fell on his head
or the ships and ships starting out aboated of themselves the
lady saying in a twang it's just like California before it got ruined
Breath
the lady saying that's the island makes this like it oughta be
Breath
and please turn away your faces from the people
out of distance out of respect out of what
it means the pickpocket looks the other way precisely
when the child's hand is rummaging like a feather in your purse)
The cartographer in this case having placed the X in a deliberately
Falsified location while you left them there
Beating heart beating heart beating heart

★

The claritas of doves bright sickening
Eula reaches out a noise receptionist
From hand to land been given troth
A trash fire brought it down
With sheep and sheep one horse whose broked experience
Wagered him to be the deft invader, city guide
And ship-arriving hollerer in one.

The substance of erasures constant signal organs
To obtain: the city must be built in this
Lithe festival of submersion, the woman's fingers
Deftly touching barracks while the leather hides
The child signals animals outside the long
Easement granted overage whilst embankment
Shirks its duties to decay—we like it this way
Said the local amulet, carving its deep flesh
With words like Eula saw each weekend day
With time to add distraction on to growth—
Then Eula took to etching ink into the hide as well
Like pen, like straw, the message self-directed
(some who carved beneath the hide detection's
willful ambulance wheeled in
our wooden carts and admonitions)

The sea orchids could not scramble in all this
Thickets without immersion—how does it feel
To own so many ships they'd ask
If but their eyes were forward follow

To the lips of soaked refusaldome
And parry legs and organs floating
Down with nothing points on them
No little stories ink-bespoke for their invisible eyes

So Eula folded her hair under the scaffolding
She decided to wait. The dawn was fulfilling
Its definition slowly in the crevice by the building's
Soft machinery. This would be historical enactment
Seen from the position of a crack.
The men came slowly folding their long bodies
In a deferential pose meant to make the sea unware
The sand watched them slowly in flat spheres
The bird flew off the tree and stood gradually on the beach
Its feathers gently sloughing off its mouth turning one way
And another till they all fell off the woman stepped out shining.
Her hair was the color of microphones, her limbs
Lithed out the inner part of stones on pulse
Her eyes unfocused glowed two screens
She smiled at her mottled flanks forbidding
(the men walked out their spheres
moved toward her cautiously unsolved)
And the flat box folded up so swiftly
Eula hardly saw what garnered the scene
And made it caution play police—
Besides the crowds were operating now
And she'd be lodged in scenery unwept
(had hardly time to seek for dream's
disparaging erasure, hardly time

imagined for this city whose divestments
were so sadly culled and fast toward
that just-enoughness impulse that would
keep the air so pale from all unbreathing)

Like the lady who lies down to open her anemone
to the glandularity of the species, Eula walks by the shore
beat-beat closed eyes *beat-beat* soft mouth internal
to the ritual adversity possession
which not-so-slowly leads us to
commiseration nation

Bulwarks

A tactic takes an order by surprise
A certain precondition (Manda finds within the new terrain)
An infidel, unfaithful acolyte, diminished sovereignty
In the crude bath and plan raids (its own position
seeming altruistic) by the mouthful
Pulling tricks it does not have the means
To keep itself, viewing blow by blow advantages
Serene cartridges, a large deployed mastery of places
Though sight does not take chances to be sure
(two figures in the art of curvature plot out
the pleasure of storytelling on the rim
of the ethnographic scale: a ruse of practices
tricks tall trees into submission after
playing story does not hold its own
tradition bath nor subterfuge
umbrella as it falls) the night in chess away
From words at all when Manda buries old ambitions

In celestial dark arrayed with composition stars
Perfume the treatise in a present that feels
Very much like the past

That is these unities surround redecorated arbor
The distributed arrangements of the tour
Inside where noblesse architectural will have its way
(one very correctly said) off in a quest
That miniaturizes the symbolic order or replicates or
Duplicates its dull asperities (these unities in one)
The function a homologous terrain to be imagined
And the fjords! And plains! And craggy creeks galoring
All those faces that speak comparable of Voice.

> *The theme of the marvelous has captured*
> *all the flowers again*
> *standing up to nature*
> *as a little child will stock and still*
> *seriously tested moralisms*
> *and their quiescently similar new ghosts*
> the threads concern us Eula
> showed defeat succeeding heart
> laid bare while impecunious shores
> erased their sentimental era
> right from under us.

We built the wall with stone by stone interiors
Admiring fashion's fit with iron's wear
And where the cracks peeked through a glint of green

We stuffed it with the faces of our enemies
In glass and practices were well prepared
We disregarded ceremony's art and peeled
Our grown-up wheels straight out to euphony

We mounted a sustained attack on every day
The proceeds from experiment stuck up stock piled
On the churches' lean exteriors where they baked and broiled
And stewed magnetic lines: and Manda strewed, and bird
and flower repetitions stitched through bark
and animals we hired making up a total man
the important thing said the tender lags
behind what we can tally plot

★

Come come let us be hither let us not pretend we are not
What we wot is the hintermost mortality can muster
The chemical advantages brewing some wastrel set
Of vigilant ontologies (that felt left behind:
they sucked their fingers and erased the messages
they'd written to destroy us into night
the night of savage-not-to-be, the not
of wisdom held suspended just above the sword we ran
the risk of seeing through)

You see the nation is agglomerate of actions brought to task
and built up into segregated wastes

we fondle through as parturition's dominant
tells us what we are is true for here we are
No renewals in the fusty value added time
no refusals of your time or attitude
no more tendrils to announce nor bold new flowers
(all our increments are underground navalized
wattled moley hillsides in announcement
pages in the back of your brave socius magazine)

We've included to add, we've added to that interjections, Manda
ideologies and rivers we can name them one way
and another we can make up time and for lost
we can size the vigil positive and no one is left out
for there they are, in the press of dead embraces
they walk through time and again over the radio
(signals we trace walk touch walk touch touch)
I can still hear them in the bold blue edges
where my chest erupts having been included
I can still hear them in the thick green where
light falls over having been included I can hear
incompleted wales push underground their furrowing
in the tally of accretion's tribe domain.

And the protesting soul always enumerates it's like this way
or that *no don't characterize don't throw*
    my obedience into your pot to stir it
    don't Manda me girl ways to straits
the ancient secrets aren't so liberating you know
those specializations don't become *I want to hold*

the hand of progress whose domestic
architectonics will dis-plate me from my gold latherings
to some non-adhesive substance that makes me
'real' unto myself or someone watching

> *(oh do watch me make me substantive*
> *knick-knack my paddy-whacks on top*
> *of your cultural display space oh let me be*
> *the speaker for the irreal let me tell you*
> *how it's going to be)*

She just cannot be quiet sometimes she is so fuel
like and irrespective you know how it is: you give
yourself to something and it sucks on you until you disappear
you invest yourself in something and the tide pulls out
whether or no you will yourself to attributes
and they fatten up until the grey line of the non-specific
horizon fulfills its disappearance, *ahh*, with an elongated sigh
whose hunger is never revealed because satiety
is it authorized appearance: here you go

Again, we are holding hands by the shore certain of our magnitude
when the boat comes in with large sashaying and we cannot keep
up we are holding the rocks by the water with our hands in pieces
next to each other unable to reach we are holding
each other's sticks in hands grabbed from the lovely waterfront trees
unable to see beyond their own
you know how it is

★

That's the moon crept through the kauri tired
Like the third text shearing frames
Heuristic lightning rods
And your castle shed near the empty sky
That sing not to another within hearing
Having landed their domestic skins with dizzy
Mattresses intact. I fell in love
With the moon's disputable mirror (solace look)
And took it to secrete my eyes and mouth, thus temporized
My Eula touched the evolution yielded up by tongue's
Proleptic fire, the smooth occasion platform
Set among the disillusioned trees
(in bud and murmur apt which having never
sutured island spaces still peninsulate
their species past request into museums
the firm hand on the knife making that easy)

We packed of course imperial sandwiches being of the best
Prime beef with cows and dotty patting sides
We patted each place down and hung the curtains
From our eyebrows (never mentioned till that eve)

When Fasti spoke the crocus petal flamed the garden fire
Irresistibly persuasive in the sycamores
    while clinging to the wisp of books
    we held down from the draft—
The ships piled in with separate rain,
Some from the sea and some from sky

The people piled sleeping sun rings
All around their new acquired houses
Built of wood to make a history of ideas—
and the dear primroses central to it all laid down
beside the gentle rivers we would cover over

Gently to announce our parley avenues
ensuite we'll huddle graciously
and breathe against the press of oral habitus
that rakes our ears with repetition's insobriety
we gall it here we lean it into threads bright red
with blood we understand (which having read about
the shedding of we know how just with grace
and gently put the mischief on our Fasti's face
who tells and tells without an actual steaming in)
all ready for it from the animals and sea, all lea.

Our mother may us strew the child, our mother held against the sky
Too many things came out until she didn't move no more
Too many books fell off the ships
Too many trees groaned consciously
Too many papers disappeared with tongues and accident
Whereby our Eula blinks to think
of how the earth turns over to no point
above the gentle flower's tippet tossed against
the water where the fish mistakes it for a spider
feast and all is in

We called it Manda stream those days and not so long ago we called
Out ankle-busting footlogs underneath our barren feet—
We called the sea by many names depending how we found it
In we called each other's voices or we carved
Out through relation busts to rival Fasti's logs.
Our we was quite expansive it could cloak and veil
The little forest floor and all the way atop of
Trees we never saw up close although we sent
Our little birds to speak to flowerlets and berries and
To bring back news

The news was never far from here, was never different but twice
And twice-told made our fronds lilt up
And twice told made us hold the ground
Our roots dug in the best they could
and licked the veins of earth

But Fasti had no time for that, no time for bunk-wheeled castors
Nor their titmouse slow velocities, the women heaving back
Their sacks not-quite-submitting to the rack
(but heaven's church was thankfully
diluted in the route—we kept the ship
dismantled there for building all the naves
and they were plasticized eventually and safely
tucked aroadside where nor import
nor no magnet drew us toward) but happily
with milk the cows and children swayed
in mountains like the grand ones promised one

no longer back no longer home at all eh Fasti
bleak your ta was all important as you sloughed off
monumental thanks from the gladly departed
the crow sang high on the head of your falsetto
land disappeared from your eyes as you strained

For the hefty wooden hull that's bound to let you go
(the price it paid in paradox eventually) self-cancelled
By the interests it could serve: oh laud that cracked-up paper
Laud the almost-vellum we can use to keep ourselves
Pro-servum, pro-domesticate

But there's always sides to every story, nay the swollen hillsides
Nay the sheered-off vista pa we're looking from, eh wot
My fambly, my amanuensis following the crack over the rocks
Where laid the scurrilously perched umbrella that we brought here
In memory of our founding Fasti, foundling of th'empirical demesnes
We scavenge through like yellow-headed birds surround that rock
Maw maw so beautiful in spite of sea's mistake and loosened
Bowels heaving down the stone—so many of them, how do
they contrive to make the nation-state reversible?, how do their
wings land steadily on the rock they've breeding carved by years?
No doubt beautiful, no doubt they fly up closer asking for some
tidings some real contribution to their remaining late
but Eula finds the press exacting though the camera hovers
steady hour by hour from far away, after all a non-diminished
stare sent down the asphalt to the penetrating eyes
(assizing wake, penitence, holdings, and this year's fine brood)

★

Twirl your doxa round your fingers
Twice without a dread
For the man in manumission
Seeks to speak: he's found his message
('who here can arrive without priority')
Speaks?, or sets up for a docent quantity
Beautiful in his togs a log on which is writ
(a script on which a script has designated animal paws
and bylaws immaterial, the kind of soft
sloth dew birds recognize when they are on their knees)
A map that's it in false material dregs
Supped down for Fasti's quotient: one knife grown dull
One primogeniture guile log
Several pictures drawn from ash
Found round the constant boats, one deed
Taken from a tired declaration that previals
A bottle reading Tincture of Time, Recollection's Immaterial Dew.

The press of such had spilled over the borders
and into the fall river empty run-down intersection of a city
reassembling stumble's stun: thy will be done
in careful avenues unsuturing the glass slipper from a dream:
an acronym has textured us into the open after all
so far from purple soft clusters of baby people looking some
direction they might tumble to in rigged-up boats they spoke
of straight to Eula who was listening:
    A falcon strewn with roses whale
      a flag bedecked with leaves erect

A simple calculation stars
a written letter made-up
love acquaintance open field
and hardened edge that broke my wheel
A pattern in the sand that led a ray
straight to my head a hand-
held manacle (instead of love)
of family branched my eyes my limbs
geared up my neck turned back
I heft the land inside
my sack and flewd.

Three parts to the event before we called it that: a plea
a look a rival. A book of trees. The loss of whom adored me.
The land whose stories very soon diluted mind

Then I was in a garden.
The looking of it made it nearly mine
Like hover pictures over their own subjecthood.

The silver moon uncovered plum tree persons
C'est pareil I was then told to separate the parts are from
The whole of the adventure comes upon you.

The years borne over now I'm thrifty dead
I tell you to restore your broken wedge: keep being the nearly-kind
Near-kin expectant forecasters you're made from
Prodigies of right-protected views encased in
Barrel laughs, a clan of mountains hovering all round

The awe-filled sails and being it abuts the Eula thinks
all states are wild and this one no exception though it
thunderously keeps arriving

★

How do we teach them, Manda thinks
meanwhile in her little wooden pages torn
with grit the children seeking nothing
further than a Safety Zone, the books with articles
about watercoloring she thinks it likely they will learn
from this she gives them lessons in the hues
they tear the paper stomp the brushes with their feet
they scream for milk they miss the land their mothers
look to while they perish in petition's lonely turn.
The mothers mothering themselves they waste
the mountains green with tears they heave the bodies
of their children into caravans they yearn for letters to prepare them
for the watercolors they'll be pictured to.
The children stare ahead of them at yokes of avenue
they put on jeans and t-shirts with the kind of fury we reserve
for mountain lions savaging the goats. The villages put on
cafés the features we reserve for repetition's callous salvages
the minister guides his flock of sheep over the hill
morning and afternoon. The bartender polishes his glasses
afternoon and evening. The mother polishes her plates over a large
supper of roasted babies. The mountain gives off
the kind of smoke usually reserved for natural fires
while the battle rages over who will most
securely husband all the slaughter.

The children grow and peel back forests they grow
And trounce trees they drink up the water in the ocean
And spit out salt they drink the blood of their lovers
And declare themselves wed they rub their faces in the
Dirt from hills and shave all their hair replacing it
With grass torn from the mountain they build up
Libraries of images to see themselves they gloss
The images with words that situate their times
They try explaining, they try driving they try swimming
Ironing diving they collect rocks shells birds paintings houses
Houses houses they collect drawings of mortgages
On their walls important meetings they attach
Their own diagrams to the average of their forebears
They erect statues of their dead selves in the image of
The living they apply for mercy help admission
To the local universities they set up against each other
In a tribute to uneasy situatedness they find in what we
Cannot recognize as Love: meanwhile the ant
Admires its feathers pasted on by children
Meanwhile the ferry is mistress of her passage
While the empty north head bunkers are hollow
With the promise of a future disposition when we'll put
On our gumboots and tromp out to sea. We've realized the end
And patience all got out of time that bottle Fasti saved
For us the purposeless the purple ones we're wasted
We're each other in our lighting levels visual sweep by
Francis Towne (who was, we haste to add, never new, never here).

Landed gently

Well it's been a week and we
look out the frame where soon
a window to the sea—from there our eyes
will sweep to see the breach that made us
follow here a moon or tidal retribution modes

the sea, the glass will soon arrive and we
insert it careful mottled end
just like old times in dimpled cogs
with little animals surrounding little icicles
for something one expects such modes

the sea. I scanned it fine
and still it made up motion's brevery
counting all the beads foreshortened
pillows. The children on the way we start
again in writing (any willing parcel wrap

to hand) bereft symphonics and our ads:
come thither thou lithe molecules, give up
your war-torn ways your lawyers yearning to drive taxis
stable masters yearning to heave youngsters here
your weak-suppressing billy-goats of old
beliefs who'll succor your succumbing offspring
in the poisonous bandanas of your clots—bright red
we hear the orator, bright red he files us past
with paper flung against our feet the oft parade
the slightly noticed willingness half-pressed
new idea corrupted in the carpets that we brought along—

I didn't know the trains would falter, feet fall
on the rocks I didn't know the clearance time
would be determinate, I didn't animate until we'd put
on every corner of the islands every woman's curve
brought out in nude surrender, we have names for that
we counter name re-name we come up wondering
which taxi ride will be our own
which gentle slope

★

A nice enough city do you know they made it shudder in its dark
green trees by fencing off so made with light and chisels
in their hands the bodies sweating at the furnaces
along the eastern shores oh can you hear stupendous gaze
along the felt land crossed from swell to monument
overhearing nations crest with ambiance we borrow casters flag

the fields with vanity in several schools and paralyze
creating pulse in ravage procreation, pulchritude that we
offset we built from scatter scratch we held the papers in
our aromatic bodies (swallow swallow) on the dirt that packed
like ramparts molding granted forms my children, my children,
how have you taken them and where, across the seas
that might as well be land, across the land that might as well be seas

And Eula of the war-torn country founds herself
unbuckled from the booth, she finds flounder in the marketplace
she pays for it with nothing that's the country we all love
    say mens gone hither
    she bounds from corridor or re
    demolishes her pleasure pa
    scrambling in the distance up
adventure. Admonishment's a windy task that someone
takes eventually rectangular in buildings and a tithe—
you know you have to work for someone willingly
to make a smallish puppet self to veer on beaches
where she smiles with clay and paste
galore she heaves new babies out

    A minimum of forty personal words
    (in a condition of rest) my father ate all the bananas
    drank all the beer and was delighted—would you give
    tame confidence the standard girl behaviors
    we keep universalized for later use?

Nay gentle shepherd still thee now

The red unravished lips of thine dependents

Still the blade that soars through space mythology intact

To know each bushy pass of this shroud land

Nothing but what's natural and common

Here grains gather from the sough

And jars of barley having now society enough—

Still gruff the settlement that leaves us sore

Thine honestly remembered tapestry whose fell edges

Would inscribe the letters that your memory holds still

If it weren't for whales we'd never have fishes if

It weren't for frangipani we'd rebuff all the conquistadors

If not for serious conversation with the European goods

These subjects would have entirely no end

In spite of laws and divine maxims the rocks are still bleeding

Surely history can present unnoticed corners where

Our councils cannot simply end despair

With a great deal of ingenuous candor

Civil restitution paints in other hues

To woo you simply sally to

The integral life, the keyboard calm

Canoes wrought architects

Happy in their docent quid

A senate house café infers

the arrival of that new intolerate voice

a girl whose story will inveigle all

the smote-out trusts five hundred years
before having an earlier blending quality
with the known—her name's an article
to frame us now, a good design
a creek a landing prow could never
disinherit the never merely boat again
called number seven waits for you
your mitochondria giving up a newly winched
posterity whose ladders take the window
where your glass-baked eyes are free
as in available as in breaking panes at curfew time
no matter what the provenance of
your houses

Dishonest shapes avail us not in this computed hour
Where my fingers fly over newly stitched cadenzas
In the breezy tactile fever of the sub-prime—
The glass in this old windowpane has trembled twice before
Nor made us any more of culture's children—
We disinherit chaos in our cold bank bows decision
Made in all our favors (though we spare individually
thoughts for those who having tied their lives
to foundering floats upon their bloated ruminations
go serene so's we don't have to look at them)
She lets her wings grow long, she lets her hair frond
Fecklessly

All the blood in my body wishes heartily now outrageous
usage calls out Eula at high-water tide now rambling what

a place we're in attempted past all help appearance
giving up the usefulness of all these men we took aboard
At once awake on hand and foot inured
how charming a perpetual feast of silent air
how invisible the southern swelling architecture
of our roll, I mused on comrades stave the boat
We lost her as we came.

Naturally heirs apparent lose their tongues occur like
waves and non-accumulating tension naturally they
want to love each other presently and not commit to
every wooden wall between themselves auspicious
circumstance will embrace the causative structures that
allow for ideology in the first place

Naturally we no longer hear that sound even when our
radios are far up into space with limbs triumphant in
the voice of the woman is the care she cedes to no-one
naturally climbing the next within the eggs she lays and
hatches in each other this structure is an ornamental
seizure for the Fasti caught in hatches own allure, his
hard and clement fissures never so certain as

Naturally what is lost is what we'd have to yield our
names and call sister brother mother father child, sea-
tender, mind-brooder, sand-counter, bird-leader, herd-
endurer, leaf-gatherer, whale-shooter, immigrant youth,
sober sustainer, free baby, world-renouncing dreamer,
cloud-watching post-successive non-accreting brain-
inveigling doom-calm yeay-say sad-eyed so-it-is one

Naturally such matters move in waves, and the bodies
of those heaped through the water bump gently, sad
if you say so, your broken heart is latched to their
interiors, sad if you know so, the lands are moving
slowly toward away each other tending arguments
against the gentle trees that stir in books we hold with
winds upon our faces from the buildings sway

★

The black sands of experiment paved
a happy trial quite by accident
I spent my first contrivance there by pulling my raft
ashore inheritance country
declining south with second thoughts
sewn in the northern-misted Jack
who racks us still.

And lying soft enclosures gently died and overdied with story
Fettered to our non-selves helpfully
glorified by crumbled sinews rapt—
my skin whereon had lain the pacts
of dubious eternity could now be fired
and replaced with red-drawn still
My boat whereon my task whereof the newspapers where
Eula walks apartment blocks are really much the same
though spinning treacherous lures more pale
though in another country.

A little history

A bad day for the newly multicultural geneticists
Keyed to spell on intake—it's a sad day when the little mistakes
Start reading Shakespeare's beard point to themselves—
We've a task on hand when weather settles us in bowers
Inscrutable, our policies floated down the nucleate shore
A child's expansion to the unknown mind
(I'm not resigning to the blue jug after all)
Rose in the goal just happened one bright morning
Bulb in a jar and her sweet face blinded by
One-worder absences
(*though he keep looking through the papers*
he keep by the alphabet he show his complete
devotion to the semi-circle August makes our time)
The rainy seasons mastered our imagined wicker
Fire-starter battles winked before you—we could sleep
And after all that time in transit it was time too.

Eula is a caring carving figured on the rocks
of her substantial inability to die—she took her tat
and adzed it through the rockface
of the boat she knew she'd go on (such a way
as you can't see your richest promontory caught
by top cartographers afloat you can arrest
the god-like habits of most anyone)
with the right condolence festival white horses
furniture and bright resplendent beer
you find you can attest to continuity's soft feathers
when you know the leopard island was his own

Keep all the animals alive as long
As boats float through with riches
Keep all the girls alive as long as someone roots
For them keep feathers trailing down the manifest
Expanse aware of all the dirt
We can breathe saved for forests
To eventually call by name—

Where Eula took a job tool-molding
Made-up tales attached to color-coded
Plates put up right next the aforementioned trees
(whence sorrow-buildings hung themselves
and little houses pulled upright
and wrapped their leather furnishings
in plastic against the salt sea's ammunition
plight in being, leopard's larger vast

pavilions left to plaster their dry tongues
against the splashing on the rocks) but
Leopard's tragedy's remote, the island grows
Grand houses out of kauri furthering opts
Sweet permission belts its trap-songs
On the labels Eula makes for them
(while she tuckers on the birds and lives
in boats afloat unmoored in case of
patrimony's hoards come gathering)

She hides upon the island where the leopard's bones
Adore the flames, the sensi fire her mind
The gates are shifting where the species
Cannot grow again, tattoos that disappear by day
And rearrive at night their quite magnificent
Alchemical cards the blown glass of the bottles
Shattered years ago in bust-exploding whims
(the satyrs eked the place, a well-accommodated
festal day the queen's announcement making
all the papers fret from feeling left behind)

The timber in question disposing the store
The public pig-shipped hundredweight
The missionary powder pound
The native sawyer head the board
He axed in utter afternoon our property a little longer
sickly daughter's harmony brought
regulations too

Seven ugly horses wanted nothing more
than waste to fire and lime
their musk and askes
lavishing a bad idea flat
against their untormented hides
so we the horses arguments
have found ourselves the kind of stories
whose demented appetites
are fore and aft

Society's a quantity of having to be cleared
we very soon gave way all admonition
to the punt—why am I in this fashion always
having the remote in hand, the scurry factors
lazy dogs and misconstrued arrivals?
How has it, lord of oceans, that
It takes so long to figure having laid the sky-boy
Straight upon the unresisting land
We cannot get them to agree? How is it we
Decide agreement's festival is one?
How can you not adore me singly dew she
thought as aspirating ashes on the garden
dusk at home and on the midnight ship

★

The man is hit in back like plate on board
when Fasti reads the newsprint fete

—a roundabout he's crossing over knowing it's not real
because the news cannot be happening—he reads
against a time whose lapse cannot be looped
or lopped off an adjacent slip
or craned across the new-made skyline
properties of aim and set
and escalation's fury Jack

The boats are moralistic now
with strong arms towing pedigree
whoever leaves us cannot know
the beehive dispositions of our where
we've heard invincible the edge of nations
true delicious inside wares the Eula poles
whose hidden stares make all
our heads suspend invisible ropes that twang
us back and risible stares are
serious as though we could imbue
dilutions in hieratic state.

With fish and chips the flyer said we'd rank our better news
One float gone down, a bureaucrat consuming
Ocean views from having eaten virtue and her
Non-consumptive twin we find ourselves
Digesting self-eluting mordant skin
'Delicious' said the article
(whose edges copped on shore
the little boys each other hoard
the little trees each mother bore)
The rocks inside your stomach groan

With having gripped their time
Beneath the greeny parchments find
We carved a growing party line.

Robed students with their books don't shy
From asking meaty questions:
If Christ is church and flies
Whence come the birdless lectures?
If we obey the law by lurch
Does chemistry make powder poof
Explode us render orthodox?
Such quests you know have foundered us before
On Fasti's quotient, with all of us fit on a pin
Parbuckling the ocean, with angles
South and north we half-expect our houses
Gorse, we half-explode our crux remorse
On everybody's bodies—*Christ give us portions*
Mandelay, Christ give us barley water
My marriage day is on its legs

and straddling the stream, I cannot hear
the men arrive with hoax and middle dream
(it's only over there they have official names for live-death
or death-life going on in spades, the ripe and stippled ranges
I've pasted across my skin, the weather has deranged it
and skies are fast on throat announcements
barely tended, the clouds amass) and then our questions
end with sticky raindrops—I think it's blood
come from the salt-heap mountains that have waited

a treacle treat, a windy seat my daughter can't abide
she swings her legs on
down the side.

★

Don't be discouraged by jagged rock
Atlantis Hekla Montserrat
The postcard views are sunken form
Of Mauna Loa's kindergarten
The Grenadines are stifling whales
The mackerels are far below (I mean deep as
A tint of rose can hide beneath your skin
I mean Southampton's transatlantic planetarium
I mean the firma terra cotta Lesser Antilles
Remote outlasts the pampas fjords
the spleen-deciphering
river gorgeous
aquamarine performing
depth of Manda's lazy eyes)

Blue Ridges Capsize Sails We Woot
(as closely following on the news)
Another Greatest Man has died
In contact with the monolith
(he actually rusted when it rains)
(he actually leaves ideas lay)
(he prime to oxidation's furrow and
scoliates our morrow)

Families picnic on the grass
a trio of black chadors pass
a river of itinerant rolls has pitched
its tasty munching here
I think I'll sit while shallow times
degree of risk appeals to us:
unmake yourselves and from the husks
make history your wanderlust, install
a program of rewards whose endgame
is a poster boy for black esparto at its ease
and loading up unpromised land.

Your complex arabesques are sweet
the zoo exhibits us as meeting all of the requirements
for food someone might eat to feed a brood that people
of the forest make because their lives are no mistaken
huddle by the water pipe, no friends of earth
can give us what we desperately don't need—
a book of answers, of succeed, of Who's Whose
Done Experiment, of blank hypotheses
that someone's bound to unemploy

We're capitally friendly to each other's busk and drill
the hoards will wait the trees will grow
the earth will spin and then we'll know
It's Christus Allus dopesy doe, fishies funfest
far to go, dark sand wallow and green tree watching
and bridge of anger to Hokianga.

All the buildings made of voices

One never sees so much as through a shutter
I dip my tongue in water just to speak
Collected stories joined inside her body
At night she sweated language on her sheets

The window by the sea-port
Is heavy with perfume
The glass mask of the woman's eyes
A key we fail to recognize

The man clears his throat in the back of the room: doggerel?
I asked them everything free indirect, and they galvanized
by stealing my freight. An art in bird time
caressing your eyes toward domination
or a trenchant ballet put on by visiting children.
One answer is that we cannot though text as text can.
Language is a reproduction forest where our bodies move

in the dark, having stayed up past our bedtime to prove
the bush is a complex device used to hearken self-consuming
interiors—hark the tui rises with perfume, the clock answers
with a solemn understanding. If the architecture of the new
room means anything the answer lies less.

What kind of experience are they supposed to have? Eula turns
the spatial rhythm of Fasti's ceremonial body. Its outlines made
for stairs uneven bank to marble set. Her city
skateboard wheels come off when she reaches
concrete blunt on sirens yawn, the physiological function of unity.
There she blows the dust off through an ollie, the small wheels
truck to coping the vast investiture of a moment's alarm
felt dire need delicious, felt on the simultaneous
technology of her hands on stet
it would be wrong to see untheorized buildings yawning to her
it would be wrong to covet bender glass race point class age
cage smoothly *the sand lies under the pavement*, Eula biding.

They being bring on time continuous
the moment founded and belief
They being shade royal ultimately
reckless springs on wheels
They having there imbibing
private nation building brew

> (Among the many bunker households there are silicate
> caretakers whose activated measurements are very small in

fact your soldier brother is in good hands your decorative
scheme has him in Sussex Opphem bastionette Octavia
important old new York)

They being broken amidst this finally found themselves grown up
To the counting hours, to the sifting through of fine cemented
Grooves where eyes in task can win you
To experience after all, the solid dry rocks
Lovely giving way to dripping caves, the metaphor creeps
Slowly through the fronds to peek at your industrial character

This sort of narrative city is what it's all about
I mean the proscenium arch can be anywhere
a tension in the broken arms that built it repeating
it isn't really windows stripped down simplified
she thinks Eula constituting people didn't know
the boundaries of their pleasantness, the libraries
shiny curtains flaxed on wear the bird
demesnes that lead us: choir, chorus, caritas, shiny stumps
on wheels, the bird having arches platform fashions
white tomatoes in its nest to stand for what
gets unpeeled when we really mean it

★

And to what does Fasti look when he needs to tell time in
the largest sense—he turns his head to the skies to see what
patterns of iniquity brought his forebears out of a quiet
straitening to this end

or he looks behind to check what words are scattered on the
ground to mark his way back or what birds will pick those
words and chew them thoughtfully and disgorge things for
their chirrups back at nests

whose fetters he can't understand because he left behind his
cudgel mask and can't get at the basic mysteries that guide
those birds in their half-emptied prayers and then he looks to
the side and sees

someone next to him whom he cannot understand and feels
coincident with that and the slope of forgetfulness comes
uneasily over his boon companion and he turns the other way
and sees

some heterogeneous substance that defines him by its presence
but he cannot fit that either over him nor exactly located on
top nor underneath even if it is genetic or general because the
offertory told them so

one time he turns again to look in front of him and can see—
nothing, a vast blank space where providential management
should be if only he could see it, if only the scaffolding of
exteriors were left on board

like the woman who walks around town with blueprints on
her face unconscious salience to tell the architects of that
particular urban space what they might have aimed for
when

they welded their ideas to trees and sand and rocks—in
short he is unenlightened, the drink does not fill him the
food sits uneasily in its shelters and his closet where he sits
at night to pray

(having understood that wood divests itself of wishes
swiftly to the invisible atmosphere) he gets in there to pray
and is no closer to anyone nor to ideas than the day began

He tried to tell the story of that feeling
to his mother's grave who listened patiently but
she could say nothing nor alleviate his sorrow—
though he understood she was the repository of
a feminized spirit unalloyed, fleshy maternal perfect incomplete
embodiment of what the papers said he was supposed to know—
he knew she was that and her replacement, her mechanical other
was meant to steer him in that direction too
but he found they couldn't know anything at the same time
what he knew and what she knew kept slipping in comportment
though she was better in the quietude of material
death than he could ever hope to be

So he would start that way, turning in different directions,
naming them sky and solicitude and by-my-side and what-I'm-
supposed-to-know and he would beg in regular intervals to
check them in

himself as though he were the big hotel on the corner
and every room could take in those ideas if it opened

up, the stones opened, the doors of his personas yielded
temperately (for it wouldn't take much, would it?

he could ask those questions and each room would reply
with a kind of concord benefit every day at tea they
would all speak together) and then he'd know

That was the energy survived him every day
helped him repeat the words he meant to say
with more deportment (well, the way he understood
that meaning more a matching-with-himself than he heard
any of his mates lay claim) he'd say them nonetheless
and get a little closer so by tea time he could feel
a sympathy with the at-onceness of people's understanding
a relief that social consciousness could be achieved
just by being exhausted in the task

But Fasti would be young only so long
as he put his feet in water every day, in the ocean
whose dire solicitude for his person extended to chilling him through
and warming him by turns, taking him out and
pushing him back by tides, by sending people out to swim
with him by turning his face up to the sky to rest when
he lay back, arms stroked against
the surge of ideation just beneath

He'd tell his friends after all the logs bounce
backward to the leaves whose filaments would shriek industrial
chaos he would reap the bounty of his cultural predilections

he would sweat a little as he strained the radiant animal
he would lick his fingers with a blank mind
made literal by the appointments of old age
And he would (we live on some wide point
of a toppled pyramid) never perish thought
in the stones, whistled in the planned trees
banked on dredging sands he would *revive*

★

For history is biography, a pair of lips once thought
And Eula lay in argument arranged
In purple malcontent to make the point hold true
I am two hundred years ago in alabaster tweaking
I am four hundred years ago in arithmetic seeking
Six hundred years there were, or more, or fewer
Or we adjure you think about
The language that you used to route
Eight hundred years of disappearing wings
(eight hundred years of university in drag)
eight hundred years (my wings dispersed) ago

The boat hove to at night for want
(of her bright auspices)
of brackish heavily under sail, while Fasti saved
(ideas of womanhood underneath)
the anchors with a harbor outlook, we might stake
or sore from leaning that direction yield

this juncture lean a blunderbuss (our curves)
from one wall to another ship our fealty gone
the boatswain entered the courtyard unsecured
the escaped man all alone in his wet clothes
to tell the tale

★

Meantime at the mast camp Manda stirred
the bones sighed for country
the rearranged consent was on a paper
bottled carefully for the occasion and extracted
from the ground on which she fled
seine or wood, feigned for the burial

Such marching is as adamant as your life
sewed stitched arrayed, loaded with wrong ideas
stove in your head, warrantless possessions
following each other heel on keel
as you dance amidst the rainsocked plot
your muddy mind could grow on
whilst you gorgeously palaver all the mindsets
close and closer to your own—come hither hard imagined
hard to say in this life, the blank stuff of 'knowing'
no closer than anyone is likely to accede—
bland parleys, blind missives, stoked defenses
piled one on one until (we reach the pinnacle
fair minded nation state whose every desire's to
please those waiting selves who stroved

and borrowed just to be asked
who yawned and pitied just to be drafted
into some version of eternity on earth
whose only lasts commend)
the reverb grown too ghast, the token set of eyes
are looking at you with interiors displayed
the weepy chronicles of mere difference

My hands are trembling with payoff really there's nothing
to do with it flies over my head I cower internally (though
reeking excessive wrought on out) I am concreteness itself my
hands upon the implement sweating (concrete bullets)

the city is rising up around me with ideas of itself in full
swing (I am registered in every hotel—I put my name on
ALL the registers) the blueprints have the names
of everyone who breathed here and the water

dripping from my fingertips is liquid (gelled indecision,
abated materialism) I think I can build the wood up one by
one by one

we had a straitened anatomy put on us by nature and we've
come this far so why not (*hold it hold it*) the shovel is digging
in slowly as they watch (*it's a golden shovel for the blustery city*)
it's a Golden Shovel

the newspaper faces are abbreviate they show docility
incarnate traps the beautiful face a vice next to my own

(*push the shovel in a bit more but oh the ground*) the shovel yields
entirely and the first spade

called they are waiting for this news back home (*oh one
farfetched notion here's*) the shovel waiting for your hands
sweat lightly shivering *with promises the people's faces* are
relaxed now we know where we are going

To the very first house in the very first cause
Way house windows bubbled froth wood
Close by vent the smoke internal bath
Cloister ornamental pidge clause girl
Quiet fathom curve furniture with the lion's feet
Crawling from the ship after that trip the
Other part is waiting motherly to the kitchen
Sink your hands into the covers where you rest
Your books beside you fondling them so far
And tear out a few pages just the ones in back
And put them under your head ideas of blank
Civility march from house to house you give
Your durable largess in bits while it gets
Smaller and larger both paradox and verisimilitude
Can have their way built fast

(Where was that palace where we stayed between?
The fishes and the soldiers plated us
The sands maximal walls bestrode the cars vroomed
Reckless in the single file sirens before and aft

The closing road the place in ports of reckoning
We are beside the sea on land, we are beside
The land on sea, you're summed where
All declaratives are magnetized)

The world collects itself for you
an adze and scarf waft
an elf idea of permanental want
The boys lined up to do your will
Your wishing has so made it thus
Strange flowers push down from the sky
and stick their spiklings into earth
You strand yourself between the elves
are features pinned on trap

The green it grows from sky to land
And spreads its ferment on the sand
The wineries are wintry might so supple
So convinced, the piney arms hold wood
To preach the pinnacle of sandy beach
On which smooth bones all lodged

Each tiny bit was once a house
Each corpuscle your breath intake and
Out again each blade on grain
Is mimicry of harvest till
You find your skin is on the reach
Stretched tight one break, Orion's beak
Traduced upon the southern cross
Whose shining pistels meet apart

Come to me here, sit with me now, don't pull your arms away

Don't tell me how mistakes will heal

Or fastened eyes will not congeal

On that which they have wrought

For Eula's eyes are outward splayed

She couldn't fix you if she tried

Her head it swivels front to back

Her vision side to side

The body's charge

The second volume planned to make a method
Of her spells and be someone entirely different collapsed
(though she rankled trees) the fragile jeopardy stripes
Were all along reverse of what she wrote
She found the stripes grow down her back she reached
Over her shoulder held the skin and pulled and
it would not release, not go at all

(the plan had one enormous drawback the unrelinquished
willingness of her body and its concrete universality
felt in tarps) we discover what was holding back the march
A theory of danger a theory of technique a theory of receivable lands
Materials labor needs good meet let us sum up
(he said within her head's idea) let us some to the water
Let us fresh water take the leaves await
The unrobe tending afterward

Manda as often happens she is dripping with
the salt that goes nowhere—
the sweet perfume her togs the growing sun falls out
of rows the flowers heavy in the fields adore
the air grown marvelous with consistency

Noncompliant remembering the rainbow on her skin
She turns her head and cannot see ideas
Children the trees, the land not scene away from
Boundary line, the buildings push out of ground
Their tops break soil and windows confident obtrude
Aside her arms lain on the earth, heave over
Her whole side between them, many buildings, more
Rise up and announce their inverse being
Sucking in the bodies of whole people with a whoosh
Delighted soldiering invested in the equity such acts
Lingering reflections on the increased city
City that she narrows with the lashes of her eyes

My increased signal moniker
Gels upon its frames and arms
That lather up the fulsome sites
The pity party cult delights
The trees in limbs and lambs in doves
We lavish with our body droves
We sand blast fun shop non delay
We hold each wave, we wave away
    Arc arc pa pa, latch to me now
    whilst sparrow lodgings beat my brow

whilst longboats lodge their camps on mine
my streamlined unction soft and fine
your strong arms down and back again
the birds of peace wired on my sins amen

The lingering mortality of the church sends out
its pulcherous bell the sole one they could carry
though longing to cast it overboard more than once
instead of little children bodies didn't have the strength
the wherewithal over that black blue green water so solid
it didn't look like anything could drop into or out of it,
the swelling surface over winds by winds construed
the plagiarized device whereby she knew to have
a memory of that kind the words entirely disassociated
from the winds that blew across her face
as she leaned sideways against the edge of the wall
which was like the halfway house the ship had lingered
there her torso terse circumspect with need
to find the next door that was not heavy with salt not
malodorous lingering unable to sleep
from the stench so good to put your head out of
the window that was not there

But here, by comparison so sane, so sweetly strewn
the flowers graven stones we heaved
out of the way we're paving in our myriad deformities
we were speaking to each other of 'the most important things'
we were looking over the hills at the white skin of our others

we were leaning over the hills at the brown skin of our others
we were lingering all the small trees
remind her of nothing so much as where she used to see
whose principles unstood by waste or keen, the handheld
century mark never bold
irrelevant to the wish she had today

★

Like the arc on the digital stage
That matches one hitch to another, Eula wed
Her land the stage coaches made to greet
With more than passing interest in
A room without any book?
What manner of incident has turned into
a permanent occasion one is forced to call
one's life? Do our divestments turn us
into horsemen (harness it's like this
Mondo bene, your particular erasures are no match
for the death of causality—I mean, who cares?
One extremely large example of cruelty
will serve us for particulars—the men lurching
sideways from any sense of commitment to the task
that someone else another day will say was theirs)
A perusal of the grotty scene a perfumed encounter
Not exactly like any other and yet with that gangster
Sense that gets conveyed whenever narrative plays
Matchy-match with you.

★

The Parties to the charge have pleaded civil

Courtesy not requisite for such a juncture would you

Please co-plane the various answers and assemble

Over the woods dripping with asperity to the time

We held hands gradual to the charge dismay

Dismay, lean us over the boards so we can see them straight

To finish lines, to pliable buildings of wood set upside

Down to the latitude (not thinking where we were) not thinking

The little Mayflower hovers so fine, the big rock sails

The logs roll so beautiful (not thinking where we were not

knowing even though we're told where are the bounds of earth

but have you ever really seen them? Have you touched

with your hands the unfolding parameters of blue

scarcely seeable as blue inside the bright

darkness of your hands enclosing?)

discovery is the softest word we can use in these conditions

Plea, please, plaint, plait the beautiful hair of her land

Sent soft, the majestic corridors felt stony

And allayed inside your memory caves (where new waves

Cannot see them where your clearing out discovers

Tenement futures) I swear my oath, Eula tries

Attention or inspecting the scene to make that stick

An opening statement everyone can hear

(for with you put your ears up close to this

committed paper, rustle rustle with regard)

your evidence held up to witness

winter having raffled off the jury

wrong thing laughing

he gets upset he

not far from the finished temple

forges struts with steplights

smelters photographs to the walls

the century-old difficult hammers

held up with his strong arms

gently destined to the fur and discipline

marking me he mouths

cull from the brace, one grain of sand

pushed slowly into each of his pores

by ten gradually working hired persons

while the pounding of the adze sounds

much like music

*

Our tale resumes the core the same
as in the days of Manda's swell
In earliest periods formed occluded temperature
(winds howling across) external appearances
Of the nation, subtle courtiers in private expectation
Groom the arts and warfare to distinction
Where the argument fawns seekingly—she straits
her sides to fit into the roads, she regards explanation
like a cork in the milk *what you seen then*!
A social being's staunch captive toying fitfully
Wan emblems of the diurnal calm she trots of
They to darkness mirrors unremitting curve—

In a sense residual birds have flight nestled in their crocks
Atop the cement building lay me down too soon
The letters and the fragments we infer a grand collage
Across the opiates of the trees that flake us down,
Sandwiches in hand, umbrellas up, the broken
Sides of colloquial death quite gumfy in oppressive relevance—
We came here and we weren't even invited
But so cleverly we can disguise soft hills
As being willing to retrieve us from the past
Cries of the diminished child

Birds freaking out by the wires
skeletal remains of trees gasping for breath
the lingering vegetative state of houses
mulch much made of cabbage latch parts
keeping the children safe from excess
bairns on brains they seed
they are the little cabbage kiddies

Really my dear we fret beyond imaginable
Caress and kindly notice monsters
In the city strafing for our mood
—Dusky, hungry, superb and rhythmic
Beauty little sister put up fabulous
For rent, beyond a sacrifice ask
A simple parasol demure as willing
Sand poured left against our waiting legs
(dry now, succulent as ice in the basking

winds that hold every exhalation of your breath
I breathe in take and sough the winds arising oh)

The monarchs returned in silence to the bush
where having an idea was much the same as yielding it up
our blue-stained faces revealing us as
planful admonitions arrived to some recipient plugs.
Denizens, forebears, retreating and not retreating
equally a shelter within a shelter having extruded
our lithe stomachs over our own appetites in order
to secrete them in the clay we found hidden inside
the hills. We'll lift it up and bury us as
orange and woody sprites become recycled selves
in bricks and troves, in scarves and trousers
lollipop specters nuzzling each other as the decades
pass entranced—the shade compels the body to follow it
as Jack unspheres on Fasti with a tender disregard
for the dictates of his person, born at the foot of the Atlas
as he was, not fooled in any lasting way
though these clay walls were lovely smelt
he made a shirt he made a belt and shoes
to tuck his pantaloons he stood stock fitted
the perfumes of earth held on his dampened limbs
the cooling down was hardening, what a relief
to feel so well, the inveigled solids of the hill
to be so fit to him, loving as he was the mysterious ways
of the country, ready to spend his time
a general reserve for those bright trees
who brush against the toy train as it casts.

Meanwhile Manda walked on shores to dances
They taught civilized, the cafes were dazzling in heat
Set moldings fat-cheeked chairs on which we sat
Reverberating my thoughts of the right
And greetings newly purchased citizen,
You come here dazed and post-serene to manage
Uptake eyes in needled animosity (toward the
What-you-might, failing every test of making choices) easy
Our decanters were of measurement so fine
We drank to progress incommunicable thought
Song writers wafting in the seats up front
With messages they'd learned to tell as their ones—

As far as I'm concerned, what is is must have found
Undress him for the burial without delay
Or so they said without recollecting their own stone
Brains grown heavier by minute declaratives
They cannot recognize—*my supreme task*
My strangely complicit reference my beatific ghost
Of future pensives wrecked on tarmac
That's run out of road, on lower classes imminent
Departure from the main romantic twist:
Finally the last country pulled its hills
And came up slowly with a voice
Whose companionate somnambulence
Was like a grid: so Manda spread ideas
Over all the leading entranceways
And the harvest of the future was well set

★

You see I've remembered everything

Though the corpse was settled in wax before we found it

Though the body was digitized before we found it

Though the hamstrung legs of the mountains were tucked

Up inside the rivers mostly habitual acts

Make craters amidst the sitting visitors:

They hardly know their bodies are being watched they hardly

Feel the swamp set rushes tied over their sweet legs

They hardly yield to drunk permissions

Already sun set fireside you *love most when it's nearby unyielding*

And Manda can go to bed proud

Can wake up in the morning and construe her secrets

In the carvings no one thinks to set against

The paper windows latched with foam

From speaking gentlemen near morn who find

Their meeting times confessed another culture's random looks

(He hanged himself, that's what he done

a ghastly face to look upon the bowels

wrought out the handsome clothes cursed

to the flames we press down when

we find our text construes again)

The will said *place him under books*

A thousand of them used to press

Him fast inside in the ground

I made the curtains of his hair

I made the windows of his eyes

I made a crown from all his teeth
And sit astride the missing heath
Whose portents plait my hair so fine
I'll need a thousand fingers, dear

Circumference

People don't want people matter rather
patter self on tops of pitter tongues platter
food (consumables, varietals, what is left
when we look up) to replicate each other set
on shelves to preen to lick, carouse, to tell
the same in pattern feets and hands and mouths
and eyes they dance the patter risk is risky
and the house all shaky I don't think
you really want the end you're diving for, tell me again
which way to Jerusalem which way?

★

I open my eyes in purgatory chasm, what
Amazing piles of culture are here simply morn
And tired hello my eyes and green historical love
Outended simplifield while no surrender flecks

Over all the piles, as though the sun gave up
In crystalline, electric nodes attached
To every shrapnel close

Up gentle, open your eyes to sounds of sweeping
Dusky pheromone her body in green togs
For the next erasure for metallic purpose
Strayed—I remember I said travel
With your loss angels, keep them close by
And the wave

      A tendril life neglectable
      with names forelocked in mother's man
      the tumble in the latched apposite
      lethal dawning turf

      What I mean is blending drum, stolen
      time creation wastes
      the pedigree of filaments
      we spin upon our windows

      What I mean is your particular
      ear pressed on the paper
      (wastes we spin on, fitted pipes that gear)

      What I mean is looked upon, historical
      and won, where can we go if not to here
      where beauteous green skin?

Close by you open eyed for then dimension's calling
You hello and ringing in your head
By morning simply clime of wish
The house new made, sore tangents in the barn
The swinging sound outside the sweeping in
For bombs in crevices

Close by you, sweeping singing, it isn't quite the time
For harvests, we have cleared away the old books
And the new ones spring is early not defined
Close by the cat you brought with arms the prodded
Sound of culture waking sing

Intrepid implement soft and wakeful
Calculate, how long before I'm missed?
Your arms extended all around the powder of
The real sweet songbirds far away and scat
Close by you indigent retreat, soft sweeping
Up, open your eyes

★

I wasn't too contemptible—did everything I could—I weren't salvages,
under that—I tried real hard real—that was the circumstances under
which—we tried and tried—we were the soft braces around the winter
trees—the birds sang innermost our coats we held them—we weren't
even whispering it was so quiet there—the fronds against our faces
tested—every ringing was the next we—told each stories to make
the time—it was so fine, under the conditions and—we were all we

were there right—each other trembling, our clothes symbolic travesty
underneath our tremble chest were waves—

Further reading

Sylvia Ashton-Warner. *Teacher*. 1963.

Jon Binnie et al, editors. *Cosmopolitan Urbanism*. 2006.

Iain Borden et al, editors. *The Unknown City: Contesting Architecture and Social Space*. 2001.

John Butler. *The Journals and Correspondence of the Reverend John Butler*. 1819–1823.

Michel de Certeau. *The Practice of Everyday Life*. 1984.

Julio Cortázar. *Around the Day in Eighty Worlds*. 1986.

J. Hector St. John de Crèvecoeur. *Letters from an American Farmer*. 1782.

Daniel Defoe. *Robinson Crusoe*. 1719.

Janet Frame. *The Pocket Mirror*. 1967.

William Henry Hunt, Richard Philip Grossenheider. *A field guide to the mammals*. 1952.

Henri Lefebvre. *Critique of Everyday Life*. 1947.

John Milton. *Comus: A Mask*. 1637.

Marco Polo. *The million / The description of the world / The travels of Marco Polo*. c. 1298, 1310–1320.

www.ingramcontent.com/pod-product-compliance
Lightning Source LLC
Chambersburg PA
CBHW022200080426
42734CB00006B/517